HELPING CHILDREN TO PRAY

Ruth Cardwell

A GRAIL PUBLICATION 1981

Also by Ruth Cardwell
Twenty Masses for Under-Twelves
Fifteen Celebrations for Under-Twelves

Price £1.90

ISBN 0 901829 59 5

© The Grail (England) 1981

Published by the Grail, 125 Waxwell Lane,
        Pinner, Middlesex HA5 3ER
Distribution: Grail Centre, 1066 London Road,
        Alvaston, Derby DE2 8QA

TO THE CHILDREN,
parents and catechists
of St Luke's, Pinner.

ACKNOWLEDGEMENTS

The Grail wishes to thank Paddy Rylands for the time, the work and the loving concern she has put into helping us to put this book together.

Ruth intended to include a section of the preparation of 'readers' which she felt very strongly about. This section was only in note form and has been given its present form by Mary Grasar, of the Grail.

The Grail expresses its gratitude for permission to reprint the following copyrighted material:

Extracts from 'PRAISE' Songs and Poems from the Bible retold for children. © 1979 A J McCallen, published in 1979 by Collins Liturgical Publications and reproduced with permission.

Extracts from YOUR WORD IS NEAR by Huub Oosterhuis. © 1968 by the Missionary Society of St Paul the Apostle in the State of New York. Used by permission of the Paulist Press.

Passages from the GOOD NEWS BIBLE, published the Bible Societies/Collins. © American Bible Society 1976.

We have been unable to trace the copyright holder of the quotation from Daniel on page 66 and will gladly acknowledge it in future printings if we can.

CONTENTS

CHAPTER 1

A Prayer Journey

'If we have taught them to pray, we have taught them everything.' In the last few years I have come to believe these words of Tillman's, whereas when I first started to teach Religious Education, prayer was just one of the topics on my syllabus. I now see it as crucial, the very heart of my helping children. To say where I am now in my teaching it seems that I need to give some account of how my own prayer life has developed.

When I was a small child I was taught, as most children are, to pray to God. I was taught formulas which I sometimes prayed thoughtfully and sometimes rattled off to God up there in heaven. He was a benign enough person, bigger than ordinary people, ready to listen and ready to give me what I prayed for 'if it was good for me'! I loved and feared him. There were occasions when I felt his eye watchfully upon me, especially when there was no one else around and I was up to no good!

I remember in my teens listening to a priest who said that God never took his eyes off his creatures because he loved them so much. His eye was not a watchful critical one, but a loving eye which 'saw what he had made and found it very good.' This was a striking idea and comforted me a lot.

When I first started to teach, in my early twenties,

I had a class of eight and nine-year-olds and was very
much tied down by the Religious Education syllabus.
The children had to know certain prayers by heart
because they were to be examined by a priest religious
inspector; so learn by heart they did. Great stress was
placed on external signs of devotion: hands joined,
thumbs crossed, standing with head bowed, and bowing
more deeply when we said the name, 'Jesus'. I did try
to create silence before we began, but I concentrated
very much on externals. I arranged an altar, lit candles
and brought flowers, as aids to peaceful, ordered
prayer. The religious inspectors were pleased and so
was I. The children were being taught to pray and a
very serious and solemn business it was.

The children had an image, I believe, of the same
sort of God that I had been brought up with, perhaps a
gentler, less punitive one, but still a God who was remote. He was in control of our lives, but one had to
stretch a long way 'out there' to find him. We prayed a
lot to our Lord, Jesus Christ. We were very much
aware of his sufferings on our behalf. The crucifixion
loomed large; the resurrection much less so. I saw it
more as a proof that Jesus is God than as part of the
glory of the cross. Jesus was closer to us than the
Father, and he was often fused with the Father, so that
we thought of him as creator and giver of life.

One very small incident triggered off a new path of
thinking for me. It was Christine, a blond eight year-
old, who leaned forward and said to me, 'But God doesn't
love everyone, does he? He sends some people to hell
and he wouldn't if he really loved them.' I felt that I
had to give her an answer quickly so I spoke of dying as
going through a gate with Jesus waiting on the path with
arms wide in welcome.'We run to him', I said, 'and he
holds our hand to lead us to the Father. But then some
people, whose lives have been filled with self say,"No,
I don't want to go with you, to do what you want". These

people turn off the path and look for a place where they can do what they want. This place, where no one cares for others, is called hell. Other people who have loved painfully and joyfully go with Jesus to heaven. No one is sent to hell,' I told Christine. 'People choose it because that is the basic way they have chosen to live without considering other people's happiness.'

Giving this quick image to the child had a deep effect on me and started off thoughts about dying and judgement. I found this image enough for me for the time being. I was torn between this personal human picture and the other extreme of being lost in the great sea of the Lord where one is submerged and caught up in God's Spirit. I still swing from one image to the other, sometimes content to step into the sea and be lost within something much bigger than myself; at other times clinging to a vision of heaven as a super-earth where all those I know share the glory and happiness of God, recognizing and relating to each other.

When I am talking about death to children I stick to the personal picture of Jesus meeting us and taking us by the hand to heaven to meet the Father and Spirit and those we love. I do not tell them that it is like that, but only that I, when I think about it, think of it like that. They will work out their own symbols for dying and death as their belief grows.

I have for some years belonged to an inter-faith group of Christians and Liberal Jews. When we discussed life after death I was impressed by the strength of their faith in the living Lord. They believe that they live on in the spirit and mind of their children and of generations yet unborn. Their idea of life after death is different from ours and yet I could accept it; accept that the good and bad I had done would live on in the people I was in touch with, my family, my community, the children I taught. Generations yet unborn would be

different because of the way I live now. A Grail saying
which is woven into the fabric of my life sums this up:
'To help one person to grow is to help to build the
world.' But there is a destructive side of my life too.
I am not always building others up. Some people will be
less fulfilled because of the way I live now.

I feel this conflict particularly with my community
whose lives are so closely enmeshed with mine, but
also with the children I help to prepare for the Sacraments. I am concerned that the God I show in my rela-
tionships with them, the God I describe when I teach,
the God I help the children to pray to, is not just a
grandfatherly figure, but has something of the power
and strength that I have come to find in my own life. I
am anxious that the children find God more quickly than
I did. I want to give them as many opportunities as
possible to be in touch with the God in their inner heart
and spirit. What they need most of all is to be able to
pray to the God within them.

As I grew older, the benign Father God, faded a
little and I became more aware of a power at work in
the world; in my life. I was attracted by the idea of
God as the ground of my being. I began to find God as
a strength within me; to be discovered when I struggled
with inner silence, when I felt in touch with the centre
of my being, and here I found God who is the centre of
Being. It brought me a peacefulness I had scarcely been
aware of. And it was in this peacefulness that I found
not a fatherly God, although the Father image is one
which is still with me, but the source of life and mystery, which drew me deeper into myself. It was not a
passive stillness, but rather the depths in the eye of
the storm, a stillness which I reached only after battling
my way through many difficulties.

When I joined the Grail community, I was lucky
enough to have space for prayer built into the pattern of

my daily life. Besides prayer in common, I had thirty
minutes each morning in chapel and thirty minutes
spiritual reading. The half-hour in chapel I found in-
credibly difficult. I was used to praying in short
snatches, grabbing five or ten minutes here and there
but thirty minutes at a stretch seemed a long time. I
was told not to depend on books during this time, to
turn distractions into prayer and so I muddled on, chat-
ting sometimes to God my Father, sometimes to Jesus;
turning to the Spirit for help to pray. I used my imag-
ination to make pictures of gardens where I sat with
Jesus and so I learnt to get through the half-hours without too much clock-watching. Although there were days
and even weeks when this prayer was dry and barren I
kept at it because it was taken for granted as part of my
life in the community.

The discovery of the Psalms made a tremendous
difference to the way I prayed; to my image of God.
The Grail community's prayer life became psalm-centred
because of the work some of us did on a new translation
from Hebrew into English. I found myself turning more
and more to the psalms as ways of expressing my life
experience, my joys and heartaches, disappointments
and surprises, my aloneness and my belonging to a
loving, supportive group. My prayer became more
stark and less sentimental. It became more free. And
I was able to express my negative feelings, my anger
with God, my doubts about him, as well as my joy and
gratitude.

When I became ill with cancer this marked a new
stage in my prayer life. At first I was so numbed that
I couldn't pray at all. My inner peace was shattered and
I filled my life with little comforting things. I was buoy-
ed up by other people's prayers. However, one day
when I was having radiotherapy treatment, which involves lying quite still, totally alone, with a huge threat-

ening machine looming over one, I found myself praying Psalm 62.

'O God, you are my God, for you I long.'
I wept and found that I was in touch with myself, the numbness was gone and I could feel God's power at work in my life.

When I pray, still and quiet in the eye of the storm, this doesn't exclude other ways of praying. As I said, the psalms are the mainstay of my prayer life and I find that the concrete images of God, comfort me. I can believe that my life is in the strong hands of God and it almost seems as if I am back at the beginning of my prayer life when I rattled off a formula to God, the distant one in heaven. Yet it is not the same circle. It is as if I have spiralled deeper and reached God at another level altogether; a personal God yet a God who is not a 'person', nor yet a super-human who can somehow be in touch with each individual and dialogue with them from out there. He is within us, that is where we find him, in the central most secret part of our being, the part which no one from outside can reach.

I have been helped to pray differently through preparing children for the Sacraments.

We teach God to children by the way we treat them, the way we talk to them, the way we treasure them. To say that God loves and values each one and then to treat some children as if they are worth less than others is to contradict the words we use. Children, and indeed adults, learn most powerfully through experience. And so the experience of being loved and valued for ourself is the strongest way of learning that God loves us and values us as we are, knowing our failures and yet still seeing each of us as uniquely created in his image. God loves us for what we are and sees in us what we might be if we open ourselves to his love. This is what transforms us.

At its beginnings the Grail Society was called 'Women of Nazareth' and there was a strong element of devotion to Mary. Her feasts were celebrated with enthusiasm and each day we prayed to her. It was Mary, a Jewish woman, whom I grew to love; not a remote white-robed ethereal creature, but a flesh and blood person who has been through what we go through. When I talk to the children about our Lady, I emphasize her ordinariness and the extra-ordinary way she responded to life as it came to her. It is not so much what happened to her which made her holy as the way she reacted to life, the way she opened herself to the transforming love of God. Because of this, Mary can be a model for everyone. We can respond as fully as possible to what life brings without waiting for the extraordinary. Older children can certainly appreciate this attitude. As Nicholas, aged eleven, wrote, 'It's just getting on with what turns up. That's just what our Lady did and we can do the same.' This attitude to life should be fostered by all that we do as well as by all that we say and can be seen by children as true holiness.

At a time when all I had was a groping faith, I came across 'Your Word is Near', by Huub Oosterhuis and this made a striking difference to my prayer life. Here I found prayers which echoed within me as if I had already prayed them countless times. There were prayers of hope and doubt, of faith and love which triggered off in me a forthright way of communicating with God.

> 'We can expect nothing, God,
> from ourselves
> and everything that we have
> comes from you.
> We are dependent on your love
> and your kindness.
> Treat us well—
> do not measure out your grace,

13

but give us your own power of life,
your son Jesus Christ,
mercy and faithfulness
more than we can imagine
today and all the days
of our lives.'

Again at low times we need prayers to express our misery and doubt and I found that Oosterhuis often started me off. Then I had confidence to pray in my own words to the God who seems not to care!

'You are no answer God
to all our questions
you are no comfort to us
when at our utmost limit
all life seems pointless
and we can go no farther.
You are no refuge God
for all our ignorance
you do not fill in gaps—

. . . .

You let life drift
and take its course
you are not here
not there not everywhere
you are not everything
you say so little.'

Sometimes that is the only way I can speak truthfully to God. There are times in my life when that is the way I feel about God. Children, too, need prayers which express their sadness and anger. Sometimes when they pray there is no answer. A J McCallum's, 'Praise', puts some of the psalms in language which children can use:

'Wake up, God!
Don't say you're still sleeping!

Can't you see we need you?
So please don't hide away.
Look, we're all in trouble.
Don't forget us please.

Wake up, God, and hear us!
Show us that you love us.
Come and help us now.'   Psalm 43, vv24-27

Through the way we pray with children, we should
give them confidence to express in their own words,
their anger and misery when they are upset. We can
let them see that these prayers are as valid as prayers
of praise and thanksgiving. We can help them to see
that feelings are neither good nor bad. They are part of
us and we have to learn to cope with them. On one
occasion John had been hurt by Benjamin and screamed,
'I hate you. I wish you were dead.' It is untrue to hush
John up and say, 'No, you don't want Ben to be dead,
you don't hate him. You love him really. Brothers always love one another.' We have to stand by John in
his anger and tell him that we understand how he feels
and it's horrible to feel like that. Later on when he
has calmed down, he may be ready to hear that we do
sometimes have very strong angry feelings against
those we love and we have to be careful not to hurt the
person while we are feeling like that. These feelings
will go and then John can do something about it.

It seems like a contradiction to say that God is within me as a power and yet I can reach him as a personal
God too, but that seems to be where I am. I swing from
the Source of my Being to the Father of all people, as
if God were sometimes transcendant and sometimes
immanent. But this immanent God is not a cosy figure.
God is peace to be with, joy to hold in my heart, but
also a tumultuous sea which makes mountains melt at
his presence; God is life, God is the ground of our being and this makes sense to me.

15

It was all these experiences, together with what I learned in community 'prayer workshops' when we explored many varied ways of meditating, that made me want to help children with their prayer and to write this book. It is not written as a guide, but as a straightforward account of what the children and I have attempted together. It may help parents, catechists and teachers to risk trying their own ways of praying with the children they love.

CHAPTER 2

Giving Them Space to Grow

It is prayer time at the end of a Saturday class. The children settle on blankets on the floor. There is a solemn lighting of candles on the low table where a Bible is the focal point.

This is the normal order of what we do. We start with a short silence, a song, spontaneous prayers from some of the class, sometimes a Bidding Prayer or a prayer from me linked with the theme of the lesson, perhaps another silence, a repeated response, a sign of the cross, the ritual putting out of candles, and that's it. I try to give an opportunity for prayer, for listening, for being consciously aware of God, for finding space.

Everyone needs space in their lives, space to grow, to breathe, to move, to explore and discover. Nowadays there is an awareness of how much space children need if they are to grow into whole people. We try to give them not just the essentials to keep them healthy physically, but opportunities for exploring, discovering, trying things out, creating, becoming aware of their feelings and articulating them. One experience which it is hard for them to find is silence. There is no need to list the myriads of noises at home and outside which make it almost impossible to experience silence.

When I had a school class of nine-year-olds, we had a weekly silent lesson, when no one in the room spoke.

17

Any necessary messages had to be written, or communicated by signs; any movement was gentle and quiet. The children loved these lessons but I have come to see that the physical silence we were trying to create was not enough. Certainly, the exterior silence did help us to feel more peaceful, to slow down a little, to be less breathless, but, like adults, children thirst for inner silence.

My current work with children is in weekly classes for two dozen 10 and 11-year-olds, a group of 14-year-olds preparing for Confirmation, some 8 and 9-year-olds preparing for Confession, and two groups of First Communicants. The lessons for the younger ones are active, with stories, discussion, drawing, singing, plasticine and cutting out, and I aim to end each lesson with prayer. It is often a ritual which they enjoy. They like taking turns at lighting candles. They play the percussion instruments enthusiastically. For the most part they are willing to join in. The older children preparing for Confirmation pray in their own group. The 8 and 9-year-olds join with their parents to pray. The 10 and 11-year-olds have a few minutes prayer with their group. However, I often feel dissatisfied. Prayer should be more than an enjoyable ritual.

I have become more and more convinced that what the children need is help to journey inwards to find God in their own hearts. To do this prayer must involve the whole person and not be merely an intellectual excercise using thoughts and words. If we can help children to pray with all of their being, mind, body, heart, spirit and senses, then we are helping them to discover themselves, to piece together the fragmentation that life's rushing pressures often create. Then they are able to enter a deeper relationship with God, meeting him with the whole of their being.

BECOMING ATTENTIVE

Prayer is an attempt to find God within our inner self and this is hard. We are surrounded and we surround ourselves with noise and from time to time we need to withdraw from the noise around us. It is often then that we notice the inner noise, the dialogue that goes on inside. We may feel firmly convinced that we cannot pray because we are pulled in all directions by distractions.

Children are like us. They may not be so aware that they are not praying, but nevertheless the inner noise is there. We can ensure, as far as possible, that the outer noise is reduced and then we should use as many ways as we can for them to experience inner silence not filled with words and noise.

Some children may have found their inner selves but most have to slog at it as we do. We should use various ways of helping them to reach the core of their being, of becoming recollected by absorption in the essence of God's creation. Focussing total attention on a picture, a feather, a stone, a word, can be a means of stilling and quietening one's self so that it is possible to find one's inner self without too much turmoil. Once children have reached this, they are usually very keen to do it again. They ask if they can have meditation and refer to experiences they have had of being absorbed within themselves.

MEDITATING THROUGH PICTURES

When I introduced the children to silent prayer, I was nervous about the outcome and I tried something very straightforward. Each child chose a picture from a collection I spread out. Then we simply sat and let the picture 'speak' to us. At the first attempt, with the 6 and 7-year-olds, we had about a minute's silence; ten-

year-olds coped with three minutes. Then I suggested
that we told God in our hearts anything at all about our
picture. After this first session, we talked about how
we felt. Those who wanted to, showed the group their
picture and shared something of what it said to them.

That simple exercise involved quite a lot of preparation. I tried to make the room comfortable, either using
a carpeted room or putting down blankets and cushions
for those who preferred to sit on the floor, and I made
sure that there was enough room for the children not to
be eyeball to eyeball. I put a notice on the door asking
people not to come in because we were praying until...
and gave the exact time we would finish. Sometimes
the children chose individual pictures which they held;
at other times, I put up half a dozen big pictures on the
walls, and the children grouped themselves near whichever one they chose. I positioned myself strategically,
that is where I foresaw any possibility of trouble.

I led in to the meditation gently and said that we
would have a time of silence when we could 'stay with'
our picture and let it 'speak' to us. Once I talked about
praying silently and said that God would speak to us
through our pictures. In the feedback afterwards I
found that the children said things like, 'When I looked
at my picture of an owl, I thought of how wise God is
and how stupid we are;' or, 'When I thought about my
picture of the mother and baby, I thought of Mary and
Jesus and how much she loved him.' This is a perfectly
valid way of praying, but usually I leave them open to
wider options by choosing language for my lead-in
which is not explicitly about prayer. Sometimes, but
not always, I used taped music as a lead-in, or to end
the silence.

I have found it good to recognize that some children
are not in the mood to pray just at the time I may suggest. I preface the lead-in to the meditation by mention-

ing that some may not want to pray and ask them to help those who are praying by being very still and quiet. I have found that this nearly always results in their co-operation. With older ones, there should, if possible, be an alternative so that they don't have to be physically present. Voluntary prayer groups out of school hours avoid this difficulty.

I sometimes initiate a sharing among the group after the meditation. I ask such questions as: 'What did you feel about your picture? What does it say to you? What came to you when we were silent?' Each contribution has to be valued and not judged, and the children need to be encouraged to support one another and to accept each person's contribution positively.

It is heartening to realise how much the children have absorbed from their lessons in the responses they share after the meditation. Some of the following examples show this.

MEDITATING ON STONES

I have tried this with 6-8-year-olds and with 10-11s. With the older ones, we took quite some time and I felt that some found it an absorbing, prayerful experience. I took some small stones I had collected by the sea's edge. Each child was given paper and pencil, chose a stone and settled down. I talked about each stone being unique and said that we would have a few minutes to get to know our own stone. During the first four minutes the mood was set by listening to music. I chose a cass-ette recording of Myers' 'Romanza', played on the guit-ar by John Williams. The next four minutes we sat in total silence. Some children were restless, more inter-ested in other people's stones than their own, but grad-ually they caught on. Soon they too were absorbed in the stone they held.

Next I asked what they had discovered about their

stone and invited those who wanted to write about it. I
spoke very gently so as not to break the mood. Then I
asked them to be silent again, this time letting the stone
'speak' to them. After another seven minutes or so,
those who wanted were able to share what had come to
them. Some spoke, some wrote, others just listened to
the exchange. We finished by praying aloud, first anyone who wished, then a general praying together about
what we had discovered.

By the end of the 'stone' session the children had
come to know their own stone, to appreciate its colours,
shape, texture. Patty said, 'Mine seemed to be alive
and to have feeling.' Philip described his as, 'Like our
lives, bumpy in some places, but smooth and easy in
others.' Several spoke of their stones lasting for ages,
strong and hard, smoothed by the sea and wind. Some
referred to 'God being a rock that goes on for ever,
powerful and not changing.' Their final prayers were
not only about the beauty of the stones but about their
durability and hardness, about how their stones spoke
to them of life, of God. Many wanted to keep their
stones to take home, agreeing with Warren: 'It's funny
how I really like my stone now.'

The 6-8-year-old children also seemed to find this
meditating on stones a good lead-in to prayer, but for
them I used only two minutes' music and three minutes'
silence. Paul's sharing was, 'I could kill someone with
this stone,' and Andrew, very anxious about this, butted
in quickly with, 'You could get some more stones and
build a wall.' But most of the younger ones talked about
the stone's appearance and feel - smooth, shiny, rough,
heavy - with an occasional burst of poetry: 'Mine spar-
kles like stars at night.' It was after this meditation
that Sheila, a very withdrawn little girl, whose family
was in turmoil, made her first contribution to the exchange. Her stone was white with a dark reddish brown

streak, and Sheila said with great feeling, 'My stone's been hurt, it's got blood on it.' From then on Sheila always joined in the sharing after the meditations and often used this time as an opportunity to express her own grief at what was happening at home.

MEDITATING ON A FEATHER

With some groups it might be a good beginning to give the children an opportunity to play with their feathers first, but I usually hand each child a feather and ask them not to let go of it and they seem to settle down to stroking it and feeling it against their face and hands. The feathers I have collected are all brown and speckled hens' feathers and with some groups this has led on to a discussion about no two feathers being identical and then about no two people being the same. Some children have wanted to write about this and have sellotaped the stem of their feather onto paper after the meditation and written such things as 'No two feathers are the same; no two people are the same.' And Lesley wrote a double-meaninged prayer, 'Thank God there is no one else in the world like me.'

However, during the silence, the children usually appreciate the feather's texture, the firm flying part or the soft fluffy bit near the stem, the beauty of how the tiny barbed fronds hook together and their sharing afterwards reflects this absorption.

MEDITATING ON HANDS

In a lead-in for the younger ones, I asked them to trace round one of their own hands and look at the shape. I spoke of the marvels that my own hands were capable of. We first concentrated on what our hands could do. We then went on to examine our own hands, some putting them palm to palm, others flexing their fingers, feeling the shape of their nails, tracing the swirls of the fingers' ridges. We prayed silently about our hands. Then discussed what we had discovered about them, ending with a general prayer about how marvellous our hands were.

MEDITATING ON CONKERS

Conkers are among the things that children may be familiar with, but mainly as things to be used, not as beautiful things to be valued for themselves. Groups within the 6-11 age range enjoyed holding and feeling their conkers and came to appreciate their beauty and their potential. Responses varied from Nicholas's, 'I like feeling the place where it was joined to its mummy tree,' to Angela's, 'God is marvellous to be able to make this grow into a huge tree.'

MEDITATING ON A FLOWER

This worked with the under-twelves. I haven't tried it with the older ones. The 10 and 11-year-old boys jibbed at first. They said 'flowers are sissy'. But having the first choice helped and also being told that they didn't have to hold the flower during the silent time. Actually several boys did pick them up once the silence deepened and we had some good sharing afterwards. However, I found it easier with the 6-8s. Their response was enthusiastic, from Victoria's: 'I chose this one because it's blue like my bathroom,' to Sharon's: 'I said to my flower, you're beautiful. I like you.' Alistair had a tall snapdragon and said, 'I couldn't get Simon Peter out of my mind. My flower is the tallest and Simon Peter was the chief one of the apostles. My flower is strong like Simon Peter.' Perhaps Sheila's was the most heartfelt. She chose a tiny pink with a bent stalk and said softly: 'My flower says, "I've been trodden on when I was small and no one sees me because I'm very low down".'

I believe that I should support the children's contributions as much as I can, not pushing them but encouraging them to go deeper, often just by my tone of voice when I respond to their comments. When I agreed with Victoria that her flower's 'blue like my bathroom', was truly a beautiful blue, she went on to say 'I think God put a lot of blue in the world because he loves blue like the sky and the sea.' In the face of Sheila's feelings, I could only say, 'Yes, your flower does look sad and small.' I was tempted to point out what a lovely colour it was, but I felt it better to stay with her sorrow so that her deep feeling was given space and not pushed hurriedly aside. Sheila, during the year, found her own way of asking for comfort, but at the time we had the flower meditation, she wasn't ready. All I could do was stand by her in her sadness.

One temptation, when praying with children, especially younger ones whose vulnerability is more obvious, is to rush in with positive answers to balance their ideas or to tone down their aggressive feelings. We need to be gentle, giving them enough support and encouragement to move on at their own pace. We may sometimes need to protect, expecially in a bigger group, but usually the need is to value what they offer, to allow them to recognize the truth of their own experience. We need to stand back and give them space to breathe and grow, trusting that they have within themselves enough resources to develop as God wants.

The children have to pray themselves. We can't do it for them. We can't make them grow, but we can give the right climate, the right atmosphere. Then it is possible for them to become more sensitive to God present at the heart of creation; to God present in the core of their own being.

We have to guard against the sort of response to their contributions that prompts them to give the 'right

sort' of answers. We should aim at freeing them from attempts to conform to our expectations. We have to avoid comments like, 'That was good.' or 'A very good prayer.'

INVOLVING MORE THAN HEARING

We can help children in other ways besides deepening the meaning of the words of prayers. People of all ages are helped by having something visual to concentrate on when they pray and this is particularly true for children. Visual aids should be as varied as possible so that the children can approach prayer with fresh energy. Within the family set up, the visuals can be particularly relevant to the children's deep life experiences.

Photographs of relatives who need prayer such as grandparents whose anniversary it is, themselves or their brothers and sisters as babies with discussion about how welcome they were; photographs of christenings and other celebrations.

Birthday cards can spark off prayers for the child in the year ahead; or individual prayers of petition or thanks for the senders.

Holiday postcards can lead into prayers of praise and thanks.

Fruit, tomatoes, flowers grown by the family can begin thought and prayer about how we work with God to produce good things.

Children's drawings can be the basis of silent or spoken prayer about the picture or about the child's feelings in creating it.

Toys: new ones which are attractive because of their newness, or old ones which have accompanied the children through many experiences, can sometimes trigger off a deep prayer expression of the child's feelings.

Treasures brought home: sycamore seeds, acorns, shells, marbles can all lead to a deeper appreciation of the world we are part of, and how life develops in marvellous ways.

Certificates for swimming, dancing, music, judo, cycling proficiency etc., can inspire sincere thanking prayers. Children can be greatly helped by their parents' prayers about their appreciation of the children's hard work and of God's presence in the children's achievements.

The possibilities for visual aids are endless. Other less personal ones are listed below.

Newspaper photographs or headlines can be reminders of people in need.

Symbols of the Church's feasts such as shiny stars, or a paper crown for Christ the King; bread for Corpus Christi, a statue decorated with flowers for a feast of our Lady, or some tools for St Joseph. They can sometimes be made by the children themselves, sometimes prepared by parents or older children as a surprise.

Candles are one of the best visual aids. They easily create a prayerful atmosphere and can sometimes be particularly effective in a darkened room.

The Bible, either a family one or a children's version, can be a focus, especially if laid out carefully on a cloth or cushion, perhaps open at an appropriate verse or passage, to be read aloud, followed by silence, shared prayer or a short discussion.

MAKING USE OF MUSIC

Recorded music can help to set the mood for peaceful prayer. Groups and families can discover what is best for them from what they have available. For most young children, a minute or two of music is enough.

Live music played by a child or adult or group can also help to create an atmosphere of celebration and joy, or quiet meditation.

Incense is an ancient symbol of our prayer rising to

God and is a neglected source of help which school or parish might revive from time to time. A substitute used by some families is joss sticks available from many Asian shops.

The value of involving senses, other than hearing, cannot be over-estimated. Children's senses are more acute than those of adults. They absorb with their whole being and they may not be helped by being drowned with words.

CHAPTER 3

Daily Bread
and Butter Prayers

Many children pray regularly with others. There
may be a pattern of nightly prayer at home with their
family or with a parent. There is daily prayer at school
assembly or before going home from school or after a
weekly Religious Education class. It is important that
these experiences help the children to pray, not merely
to go through a routine unconnected with their lives.
Any prayer should strengthen the idea that prayer is a
response to life, an expression, a communication of
what we are. It helps us to discover the demands of life
and how God calls us to respond. Prayer sums up our
openness to God: our willingness to be transformed;
our eagerness to work with Christ to transform the
world into his kingdom.

Our hearts cry out to God, whose power is stronger
than we are. We come to the end of our own resources
and we want, and need, to open our empty hands to receive. Asking God, turning to him and actually asking
for what we need helps to keep us rooted in reality,
acknowledging that we are dependent on him. We just
cannot do everything ourselves. Prayers of asking keep
hope alive in us. We have to be ready to receive as well
as to give and unless we go to God with our hands open,
ready to accept, we may forget that we are dependent

creatures made by God. We are his created children.
But prayers of asking are only part of our communication with God. We want to praise him, to give thanks,
to worship, to admit our sinfulness and our weaknesses.

There will be days when prayer becomes routine,
but for the most part parents, catechists, teachers and
priests should attempt to make the times of communal
prayer meaningful for the children. I know from my own
experience that my praying the Our Father at Mass can
be intensified if the priest leads into it with words different from the usual formula. He may re-emphasize
the Mass theme or link it with one of the Scripture readings, for instance: 'Happy are the peacemakers. Let us
pray with Jesus that we will make peace by forgiving
those who trespass against us.' Or, 'Let us pray with
Christ who called us to change the world into God's
kingdom of justice.'

It is good for children to pray formally together, especially those prayers that are part of Mass: the Our
Father, Hail Mary, I Confess, Lord Have Mercy, Holy,
Holy, Holy. Adults can help children to find new mean-
ings in these prayers and so deepen their involvement
in the liturgy.

FINDING NEW MEANINGS

THE LORD'S PRAYER

When we pray with children we can focus briefly on
the Our Father as a prayer of praise, or of hope; or a
prayer for forgiveness or strength in difficulties.
Sometimes it is enough to have a short lead-in before a
formal prayer and then a moment of silence. It is always
helpful if the words could be put up for everyone to see.

Here is an example of such a lead-in:
Our Father: Let us stop for a minute and ask ourselves

why we pray Our Father and not My Father...
(pause)

Hallowed be thy name: Let us pray in the Our Father
that more and more people will believe that
God's name is holy, because he is holy......
(pause)

Thy kingdom come: Let us pray with hope that we shall
work to change the world into God's kingdom
of justice/peace/love/truth... (pause)

Thy will be done on earth as it is in heaven: We pray
that we shall be more ready to do what we know
is right, to do God's will here and now....
(pause)

Give us this day our daily bread: Let us pray that the
world will become a place where everyone has
a fair share of food. Or, let us think about the
Bread of Life which God offers us so freely.
Or, let us join our prayer with those who des-
perately need daily bread... (pause)

Forgive us our trespasses as we forgive those who trespass against us: Let us pray that we will become more
forgiving. Or, let us pray that we won't want
to get our own back when we are hurt... (pause)

Lead us not into temptation: Let us ask that when we are
tempted to do wrong we shall feel God at our
side to help us choose the right action...(pause)

Deliver us from evil: We can pray that we shall trust
God even when we seem overwhelmed by evil...
(pause)

THE GLORY BE

Even a short prayer like the Glory be... can have a
different lead-in now and again. These are some examples:

When we praise God we are joining with everyone and
everything God makes, to tell him how wonderful he is

31

(pause). Glory be...

Today let us join:

> with the men who praise God by working to change raw metal into cars (pause) Glory be..
> with mothers who praise God by cooking for their families (pause) Glory be...
> with those who praise God by nursing sick people (pause) Glory be...
> with children who praise God by caring for pets (pause).Glory be...
> with children who praise God by trying to be generous like our Lord Jesus (pause). Glory be

Let us praise God for trees that grow tall and strong (pause). Glory be...

Children will soon catch on to the idea and some will do the lead-in occasionally.

THE HAIL MARY

There are many ways of introducing the Hail Mary:
Let us think about the angel's greeting to Mary: 'Hail, full of grace'. Now say it with all our hearts, telling Mary that we know she is filled with God's love (pause).
Let us think of Elizabeth saying to Mary: 'Blessed art thou among women'. We can say it with all our hearts, telling Mary that she is really special (pause).
Let us join our prayer with all those who are dying and need to feel God by their side (pause).

REVIEWING THE DAY

QUESTIONS AND ANSWERS

Occasionally the evening prayer, before going home from school or at bedtime, can be a straightforward review of the day. The parent or teacher can introduce the prayer with a simple question once the children are settled: 'I want you to think quietly about the answer to a question I am going to ask. Don't bother anyone else. Just look into your own heart very quietly and ask yourself:

Has today been a happy day or a sad day (pause)?
What made it like that (pause)?
Was there anything especially happy or sad or annoying (pause)?
Could you have made it different (pause)?
Tell God, our Father, how you feel about today (pause).
You may want to thank God, or tell him that you are sorry or angry about something. (pause)
Who would like to pray aloud about the day?'
(Pause for any contributions.)

The adult then sums up the group's prayer in words like the following:

'God, our Father, for some of us today has been a good day with lots of things we have enjoyed.

Children, can you think of things you have enjoyed?' (The children make a list of things.)

'But Lord, some people have not enjoyed everything. They may have been disappointed, felt left out, treated unfairly, had to do work they didn't want to do. They may feel unwell or just generally miserable. We pray for everyone, the happy, the sad, and those who feel a bit of both. We thank you for giving us this day. We praise and thank you, Lord.'

LINKED TO DAILY LIFE

A reading which expresses the feelings of the moment or describes a given situation can be helpful and bring Scripture into daily life. Evening prayer may consist of a reading, and perhaps a hymn or some prayers based on it:

Colossians 1:3-6   (Looking forward to heaven)
     'We always give thanks to God, the Father of our
Lord Jesus Christ, when we pray for you. For we
have heard of your faith in Christ Jesus and of your
love for all God's people. When the true message,
the Good News, first came to you, you heard about
the hope it offers. So your faith and love are based
on what you hope for, which is kept safe for you in
heaven. The gospel keeps bringing blessings and is
spreading throughout the world just as it has among
you ever since the day you first heard about the
grace of God and came to know it as it really is.'

2 Corinthians 1:3-5   (Thanks for help. Help others.)
     'Let us give thanks to the God and Father of our
Lord Jesus Christ, the merciful Father, the God
from whom all help comes! He helps us in all our
troubles, so that we are able to help others who have
all kinds of troubles, using the same help that we ourselves have received from God. Just as we have a
share in Christ's many sufferings, so also through
Christ we share in God's great help.'

1 Peter 5:6 & 7   (Unload worries.)
     'Humble yourselves, then, under God's mighty
hand, so that he will lift you up in his own good time.
Leave all your worries with him because he cares
for you.'

1 Peter 3:8 & 9   (Agree: no getting your own back.)
     'To conclude: you must all have the same attitude
and the same feelings; love one another as brothers,
and be kind and humble with one another. Do not pay
back evil with evil or cursing with cursing; instead,
pay back with a blessing, because a blessing is what
God promised to give you when he called you.'

Romans 8:35, 37-39   (Difficulties)

'Who, then, can separate us from the love of Christ? Can trouble do it, or hardship or persecution or hunger or poverty or danger or death? No, in all these things we have complete victory through him who loved us! For I am certain that nothing can separate us from his love: neither death nor life, neither angels nor other heavenly rulers or powers, neither the present nor the future, neither the world above nor the world below—there is nothing in all creation that will ever be able to separate us from the love of God which is ours through Christ Jesus our Lord.'

THE GOSPEL IN THE FIRST PERSON

After a few years of hearing the Gospel stories, children can become dulled to them. Nine-year-olds and over can be jerked into listening more acutely if the story is read, or told, as if by someone present when it happened.

Here is an example. In the story of the cure of an epileptic boy, Mark 9:14-28, the father can re-tell the incident. During the reading 'I' is substituted for 'the man' or 'the father'. The story would read as follows:

'When they joined the rest of the disciples, they saw a large crowd round them and some teachers of the Law arguing with them. When the people saw Jesus, they were greatly surprised, and ran to him and greeted him. Jesus asked his disciples, "What are you arguing with them about?"

I answered him from the crowd, "Teacher, I brought my son to you, because he has an evil spirit in him and cannot talk. Whenever the spirit attacks him, it throws him to the ground, and he foams at the mouth, grits his teeth, and becomes stiff all over. I asked your disciples to drive the spirit out, but they could not."

Jesus said to them, "How unbelieving you people are! How long must I stay with you? How long do I have to put up with you? Bring the boy to me!" They brought him to Jesus.

As soon as the spirit saw Jesus, it threw the boy into a fit, so that he fell on the ground and rolled round, foaming at the mouth. "How long has he been like this?" Jesus asked me.

"Ever since he was a child," I replied. "Many times the evil spirit has tried to kill him by throwing him in the fire and into water. Have pity on us and help us, if you possibly can!"

"Yes," said Jesus, "if you yourself can! Everything is possible for the person who has faith."

I cried out at once, "I do have faith, but not enough. Help me to have more!" '

Jesus noticed that the crowd was closing in on us, so he gave a command to the evil spirit. "Deaf and dumb spirit," he said, "I order you to come out of the boy and never go into him again!"

The spirit screamed, threw the boy into a bad fit, and came out. The boy looked like a corpse, and everyone said, "He is dead!" But Jesus took the boy by the hand and helped him to rise, and he stood up.'

The reading needs careful preparation, not only to ensure that there are no hesitations at the substitutions of 'I' etc., but also so that the adult can communicate the feeling of what is happening. Some adults may prefer to tell the story in their own words, but the straightforward reading of the text can be very effective.

After the reading, there could be a question leading to silent prayer. For instance: 'What would be your feelings towards Jesus if you were the boy's father? What would you say to him?' The silence can be followed by shared prayer or an exchange of what the children felt, or even by their writing about the incident from the angle of the person who told the story. The adult should encourage the children to express their feelings: 'Yes, that tells the story clearly, but what did the man feel?'

Here are some incidents which lend themselves to being used in this way:

Mark 3:1-5   The story of the man with a withered hand as told by one of the crowd.

Mark 10:46-52 The experience of the blind man of Jericho as told by the man himself.

Mark 14:66-72 Peter's denials as told by Peter.

The Resurrection appearances can be re-thought by using these stories:

Luke 24:13-25 What happened on the road to Emmaus told by two disciples.

John 20:11-18   The appearance of Jesus to Mary as told by Mary.

John 20:24-29   The dialogue between Jesus and Thomas as told by Thomas.

John 21:15-17   The conversation of Jesus with Peter as told by Peter.

Younger children are more likely to be told gospel stories in the words of the teacher or parent. He/she too can tell the story as if he/she were someone present. Then the children can be asked to think silently, 'What does Peter feel about Jesus? Do you see him as a strong, loving, gentle, forgiving, happy, etc. person? Could you draw Jesus like that? Make a picture showing Jesus as strong, happy, etc. How are you going to show Jesus like that? Think about it for a minute before you begin.' The drawings should be done in silence perhaps with recorded music to set the atmosphere. Then the children can be gathered together each holding his/her picture and they can tell Jesus silently what they feel about him. Afterwards, there could be a sharing by those who wish and a final prayer by child or adult.

ONE WORD PRAYER

There is a very ancient form of prayer, or meditation, which some children take to like ducks to water. It is the 'one-word meditation' and it gives those who use it the chance to find God within themselves: 'You know him, because he dwells with you and is in you' (John 14:17).

To help to focus on God within, each person chooses a word or phrase to hang on to and this is repeated silently over and over again. This word is called a mantra. It acts as an anchor pulling us back to the focal point within us.

With small children, I have found it best to give them a mantra that is a word or phrase e.g. 'Jesus, I love you.' An ancient word which I also use is, 'Maranatha'. They savour this word, knowing that it means 'Come, Lord Jesus.' I break it down into syllables and write it up for them to see 'Ma-ra-na-tha'. Older children will be interested to know that it is an ancient Christian prayer in Aramaic, our Lord's own language (Cor. 16:22 and Revelation Epilogue v 20)

As with other forms of prayer the room should be as comfortable as possible with the children able to choose chairs, cushions or blankets if this can be managed. It is important to ensure that there are no interruptions.

At first we repeat the word or phrase aloud for the whole time e.g. three to five minutes, over and over again until the children have established an easy rhythm. Next time we whisper it and then say it silently moving our lips and then repeat it in our hearts, without moving our lips. Some children, however, say it with moving lips all through the meditation and this does not matter; in fact they can be told that this is one way that some people do use their mantra.

Just before we begin I remind them of the mantra we are using and that we will keep on praying with this word or phrase silently. I also remind them that if they find they have stopped saying the word or phrase they should simply start off again. I then give a gentle lead-in to the idea of finding God within us in peace and stillness. I put on some music for about two minutes and then we have silence. After a few minutes, at first perhaps only two, I bring in the music again and then if the children want, they can talk about how they felt.

When the children have had some experience of this kind of prayer, the time of silent prayer should be lengthened. One disadvantage for the adult is that, in spite of wanting to be as still and absorbed as the children, you have to be alert to the time. I find this is a block to the steadiness of my own meditation and I have yet to find a solution to this difficulty.

It may be possible to record music, then have silence on the tape for a certain length of time and then let the music come on again. This assumes that the adult knows in advance how long the children will 'hold the meditation' and this is not always possible.

The idea of praying their word or phrase at other times can be encouraged and times when it would be possible to do this could be discussed. Jerry, a tough eleven-year-old, told me: 'I say Maranatha in bed before I go to sleep. It makes me feel peaceful like when people have put me in a bad mood.' Tim used to pray his during cross-country running at school. He said that it fitted in with the rhythm of running.

CHAPTER 4

Some Worked-Out Meditations

HOME IS WHERE WE LEARN TO LOVE

(For 6, 7 and 8-year-old children)

Have pictures of different kinds of houses - terrace, semi-detached, bungalows, flats, caravans, wigwams, house-boats. Provide coloured sticky paper, felt pens etc.

Start off by looking at these and talk about what we learn in our home and then put up on the wall-board the following sentences:

Home is where we learn to love and give.

Home is a place for making other people happy. Each child has a house-shape and makes the front look like her/his home. Each writes inside it one of these two sentences.

Then ask: 'Who lives in your home? How many children are there?' Line up the child with the biggest family at one end and the only children at the other.

Pair the children off and tell them that, as at home they learn to give and to make, so they are going to make a present for their partner now.

When I have done this with the children, some have made stapled notebooks with designs on the covers; others have made sets of flags using cocktail sticks and odd scraps of paper. Still others have made cards, drawings and cut-out butterflies.

Follow this up with a meditation. You could say something like this:

'Sit quietly and hold your house. Close your eyes. (Short pause) You're going home. Go in through the door and go to your favourite room - it might be your bedroom, the kitchen or another room. Make yourself comfortable there. Look around and see all the things in the room, the things you like. Stay there and enjoy the room. (Pause) What can you see out of the window? How do you feel now that you're there? Do you want someone with you? Someone who'll be very quiet with you while you're thinking. Now talk to God about your room, what you like that's in the room, what you like doing there. Stay quietly there for a minute or two. Now open your eyes and look around.'

End with a prayer said aloud, thanking God for that room and then perhaps thank God for the house itself, for example:

> Lord God, thank you for our homes.
> Thank you for my favourite room.
> Thank you for our home, where we learn to
> give, to share, to love.

In a meditation of this sort, dealing with the home-life the adult has to be sensitive to pick up and build on any fragments contributed by children from apparently difficult homes. Make the most of any signs of love referred to by these children.

I remember the Griffin family, when I was growing up in a dockside area. The father had a rag and bone cart and ran a second-hand shop. He seemed to be always cuffing and cursing the children as they struggled to survive in their big family. Their mother told me something I'll never forget. She said that sometimes on a Saturday, his big pub night, when he came in after the pubs were shut, he would wake all the children up, collect them on one bed and dole out newspapers of chips. 'He's a right b...,' she said, 'but those kids love him especially on Saturdays.' It brought home to me sharply that I had no idea how love worked in that family. The children did love their father and those Saturday night chip suppers were highlights in their drab life which they would always remember. The fact that children are unkempt and smelly and attend school irregularly doesn't mean that they are necessarily unloved. The catechist or teacher has to be aware of the riches that those children may share at home with those who love them.

FOUR QUARTERS ON A SHIELD

The first group I tried this meditation with was a group of 10 and 11-year-old children. They were preparing for a Penance celebration followed by individual Confessions. I wanted to give them an experience of looking into themselves with fresh eyes. They drew a shield and quartered it. In the top quarters they drew symbols of things they were good at; in the lower quarters, they drew symbols of two of their good qualities. Then they prayed silently about their shield.

I introduced the idea of looking at the positive side of ourselves, especially at our gifts, and then the children spaced themselves out as far as possible, so that they didn't feel overlooked.

They drew the shield as large as they could, using big felt pens. There were smaller pens for the more tentative people, but I encouraged them to start with a big, bold shield, quartered. I stressed that we were not aiming at an artistic creation. The drawings were not going to be shown to the class. I put up a shield outline for them to refer to during the meditation. I explained to them that we should have music and then silence while they thought about what they would put in their quarters.

one thing I'm good at.	Another thing I'm good at.
One of my good qualities.	Another of my good qualities.

We had two minutes of taped music fading into silence. For most children's groups fifteen minutes silence is about right. The children were asked to help those who took longer by keeping still and silent until everyone was ready. They tackled the two top quarters quickly. Drawings included ballet shoes, footballs, a shopping bag, musical instruments, swimming badges. The lower quarters took longer. There was an ear for a good listener; a face with a downturned mouth beside a smiling face to stand for the gift of cheering people up; a smooth sea to represent calmness when people quarrelled.....

Next I asked them to sit comfortably holding their shields. After a few minutes I asked them to think over these questions silently:

How do you feel about your shield? (Pause)
Which quarter was the easiest to think of?
(Pause)
Which part was the most difficult to think of?
(Pause)
What would you say to God about your shield?
(Pause)
What might he answer? (Pause)

We ended with silent prayer and anyone who wished could contribute praise and thanks to God for the gifts we have. Afterwards, some children may want to talk about the experience and this can be valuable as long as there is no pressure to contribute to the exchange.

It is essential that the adult should join in this meditation and draw her/his shield. It is rarely a good idea for the adult to stand apart from the group. Through her prayerfulness, she can draw the children into deeper reflection, although my own experience is often that of being pulled into deeper meditation by the children's absorption and silence.

A CIRCLE WITH SEGMENTS   For ten-year-olds plus.

The groundwork for this type of meditation is particularly important. I have only used this meditation with children after they have been helped to reflect on their own lives in the weekly lessons. And I have found that it can be usefully linked with Confirmation preparation.

This exercise needs plenty of time. It should be done in silence and the children spaced out so that they are not too much overlooked. Provide felt pens, crayons, coloured pencils. To create the right atmosphere, taped music can be a useful lead-in for the first few minutes and can also help to bring the group back from their silent concentration. Give the children the following instructions in your own words:

> 'Draw a big circle, about fifteen inches in diameter (or provide paper already cut into circles).
> Divide your circle into eight segments.
> In the top four segments draw symbols of things you enjoy.
> In the lower ones draw symbols of things you dislike.

When the children or young people have done this, ask the following questions in a meditative way, giving time

44

for them to reflect quietly:

'I am going to ask some questions and there'll be silence after each one so that we can think over our own answers quietly:

> 'What is it about the things shown in the top segments which makes them enjoyable for me? What about the things I dislike? Why do I dislike them?
> Are there any direct opposites among the segments - e.g. noise versus quietness?
> Was there any difference in the way I tackled the top and the bottom segments? More enthusiasm? More satisfaction? More ease? Choice of colours?
> What can I learn about myself from these symbols?'

We now have a few minutes when we can talk to God, telling him how we feel about one or two of the segments, perhaps, or the circle in general.'

The adult may feel that the meditation should end with some communal prayer, but as each group is different, it may be best simply to end with silence. The children may like to take their circles away to think about when they are alone.

It is sometimes useful to discuss the experience of prayer in a non-judgemental way, the adult making it clear that different people have varying depths of involvement at different times. Today it may be the turn of some to have been greatly helped, for others it may have been a surface experience. We can't pray to order!

CHAPTER 5

Occasional Prayers

Children should learn through experience that prayer can be an expression of our lives NOW; that today's personal prayer can reflect the joy or pain that we are feeling at the time we pray. It is easier to help children to do this when we are praying with one child, but there are occasions when a group experience can be expressed by everyone. On these occasions it might be better to concentrate on that one experience and not to attempt to include praise, thanks, sorrow and requests, but to select prayers to express the current mood.

After a really happy day out or a special treat the group may be ready to praise God together, telling him how wonderful he is, how marvellous his world, how glad they are to be alive. If a class, or family, are sharing the grief of someone's death, or the anxiety of someone's serious illness, this too can be the main thrust of prayer that day, even to the exclusion of everything else. To focus on one thing can give prayer a power which may be weakened by tagging on the usual routine prayers.

It is helpful, whenever possible, to give the children copies of the prayers, readings and songs so that they can join in easily and also so that they can take their copies home to show their parents and so use them again if a similar occasion arises.

AFTER A QUARREL

One of the strongest prayer experiences I shared with children was at the end of a day when there had been a vicious quarrel between two of them and many others had taken sides. We had discussed it and temperatures had cooled. When we came to our usual prayer time, we prayed about what had happened:

Introduction: St Paul wrote a letter to some Christians who must have been like us, sometimes very quarrelsome. Part of his letter could almost have been meant for us today. We shall see later, that St Peter also writes something that is just right for us.

Reading: 'Do not use harmful words, but only helpful words, the kind that build up and provide what is needed, so that what you say will do good to those who hear you. And do not make God's Holy Spirit sad; for the Spirit is God's mark of ownership on you, a guarantee that the Day will come when God will set you free. Get rid of all bitterness, passion, and anger. No more shouting or insults, no more hateful feelings of any sort. Instead be kind and tender-hearted to one another, and forgive one another, as God has forgiven you through Christ.' (Ephesians 4:29-32)

Prayer: God, you are our Father.
You call us to live as your children,
to be one family, a sign to the world of your love.
Yet we make each other unhappy,
we quarrel and say unkind things.
Forgive us, Lord.
Take us as we are and change us,
so that we forgive each other
and start again.

Hymn: Lord have mercy, Christ have mercy, Lord
         have mercy, sung to any tune they know (e.g.
         the Israeli Mass, 'Folk Hymnal' Vol. 2)

         Exchange a sign of peace with as many people
         as possible.

Hymn: Shalom, my friend. (Celebration Hymnal No 276)

Reading: 'You must all have the same attitude and the
         same feelings; love one another as brothers,
         and be kind and humble with one another. Do
         not pay back evil with evil or cursing with cur-
         sing; instead, pay back with a blessing, because
         a blessing is what God promised to give you
         when he called you.'   (1 Peter 3:8 & 9)

         Let us all think quietly in our hearts and tell
         God we are sorry if we have hurt or upset any-
         one today (pause). We can now turn to God our
         Father and say the prayer Jesus taught us to
         say whenever we want to pray ....
         Our Father ....

         PRAISE AFTER A HAPPY DAY

Introduction: The whole book of psalms, 150 of them,
         are called Prayers of Praise. Let's begin our
         prayer with one which is especially filled with
         praise for God. It seems to fit in with how we
         feel today. (Then Psalm 150 or part of Psalm
         46 may be read.)

Reading: Alleluia
         Praise God in his holy place,
         praise him in his mighty heavens.
         Praise him for his powerful deeds,
         praise his surpassing greatness.

         O praise him with sound of trumpet,

48

praise him with lute and harp.
Praise him with timbrel and dance,
praise him with strings and pipes.

O praise him with resounding cymbals,
praise him with clashing of cymbals.
Let everything that lives and that breathes
give praise to the Lord. Alleluia.
                              (Psalm 150 Grail Version)
   OR
Reading: All people, clap your hands,
            cry to God with shouts of joy!

Sing praise for God, sing praise.
Sing praise to our king, sing praise.

God is king of all the earth.
Sing praise with all your skill.
                              (Psalm 46 Grail Version)

Allow a short pause for silent prayer (for young
children no longer than 2-3 minutes) while the
children think over what they have said in the
psalm.
Follow this with a litany of praise. Each child
(or in twos) could make a short sentence of
praise. In the meanwhile the catechist writes,
for all to see, a response to the litany e.g.
We praise you God, Lord of our World.
                    OR
The world is filled with the glory of God.

Hymn: 'All creation, bless the Lord.' (Celebration
          Hymnal No.3, or another praising hymn that
          they know.)

GRIEF AT SOMEONE'S DEATH

This could be used either in a family or school/parish
situation when someone known and loved has died, par-

ticularly when the person was involved with the children, during his/her lifetime. It is important however, to make sure that the children are not made to feel that they are wrong in wanting or needing to show their grief outwardly, and if this should happen during this prayer time, then stop and talk about it with them, explaining carefully that to be sad is natural and that the reason they are praying is to ask God our Father, to help them during this sad time, but also thanking him for giving N a new life with him in heaven.

Introduction: When someone dies we worry about what happens to them as well as feeling sad because we feel as if we have lost them. Here is a short piece from the Book of Revelation which might help us.

Reading: 'Never again will they hunger or thirst; neither sun nor any scorching heat will burn them, because the Lamb, who is in the centre of the throne, will be their shepherd, and he will guide them to springs of life-giving water. And God will wipe every tear from their eyes.'
(Revelation 7:16 & 17)

Prayer: We thank you, God,
for the life of N... who was dear to us
and who has died.
We thank you for the happiness and love
he/she gave to the world.
(Pause)
We pray for ourselves
who are sad at this death
and feel as if we have lost him/her.
Help us to comfort one another
and to believe more deeply
that you, Lord, stand by us.
You are with us always

and lead us to our resurrection. Amen.

Reading: 'None of us lives for himself only, none of us
dies for himself only. If we live it is for the
Lord that we live, and if we die, it is for the
Lord that we die. So whether we live or die we
belong to the Lord.' (Romans 14:7 & 8)

Prayer: All say the Our Father....
They all know that God is with them and can see
into their hearts and understand how they really
feel about N's dying.

PRAYER OF THANKS

This short time of prayer can take place anywhere
and at any time. It is informal and involves the children
in considering carefully and prayerfully, the things they
can particularly thank God for. To help the children the
catechist could have made a happiness collage - faces,
situations etc. and put it where all can see it. Allow the
children to look at it for a few minutes to get the feeling
of happiness.

Reading: 'Be thankful in all circumstances. This is what
God wants from you in your life in union with
Christ Jesus.' (1 Thessalonians 5:18)

Litany: Ask the children to think of one thing they would
like to thank God for - it can be anything, and
tell them that after a short time each person
will say aloud what their prayer is, and that
you will write it on the board/paper, so that
everyone can see. Ask the children to suggest
a response or give them one that you have already made up e.g. Thank you Father, you
give us so much.
Then ask each child to say his/her prayer aloud

and all say the response together.

Prayer: We give thanks to you, God,
for all your gifts to us,
especially the gift of life
and everything that keeps us alive
and gives us joy.   Amen.

Hymn: Part of 'Thank You.' (Celebration Hymnal No.
298) OR 'Now thank we all our God.' (Celebration Hymnal No.211)

There is something to be said for encouraging
the children to make a 'home made' prayer
book.

MEDITATION FOR ALL SAINTS DAY
(6-9-year-old children)

Have a large selection of pictures of children, cut
from magazines, preferably stuck onto pieces of white
card or paper. Spread them out so that they can be seen.

Ask the children if they know anything about saints,
trying to get over the point that anyone who has lived,
and who tried to live like Jesus, went to heaven when
they died. God our Father was so pleased to have them
in heaven, that he gave them a special new life so that
they could live happily, with Jesus, for ever. These
people are all saints. Talk about the children themselves,
letting them rediscover that they became God's children
and brothers and sisters of Jesus when they were chris-
tened. God was asking them, at that moment, to live
like Jesus, so that they too, would live with him for
ever, in heaven, when they died. Discuss how they do
this in practice. Let them give examples of living like
Jesus, from their own lives.

Let each child choose one of the pictures, whichever
one he/she likes best. Let them hold their picture,

looking at it carefully, and quietly. After a couple of
minutes tell them that you are going to ask them a question about their picture, which you want them to answer
in their hearts: 'How is the girl or boy in my picture
going to be like Jesus and then become a saint?' This
will mean that they will really have to get to know their
picture and learn something about the boy or girl they
are looking at. Give them two or three minutes to think
about this question so that it is a prayerful time.

Tell the children that you are going to help them get
to know the person in their picture, by asking several
questions, which again you want them to answer quietly
in their hearts. Use any questions you would like and
which may seem particularly appropriate for your group,
but the ones below could be a starting point.
Does your person look as if he/she is going to become
a saint:
   - by being friendly?
   - by being gentle?
   - by being forgiving, and not getting his/her own
     back on people when they have been hurt?
   - by telling good jokes to cheer up sad people?
   - by being sorry when they've been in a bad temper?
   - by noticing lonely people and including them in
     games?
   - by being good at keeping secrets?
   - by thinking of surprises for people?
   - by helping at home when their mother seems very
     tired?
   - by being kind to brothers and sisters?

Leave a few moments after each question, to give the
children time to really answer the question, and to think.
Then give each child a piece of paper and ask him to
draw himself doing or saying something which will help
him to become a saint. Ask the children to choose
something they think they could try to do during the week.

Let them keep the pictures to take home to remind them of their resolution.

Final Prayer:
Catechist: God our Father, we want to live for ever with you.
All: God our Father.... (as above)
Catechist: We want to be saints, but sometimes it's not easy.
All: We want....
Catechist: Please help us, especially when we find it hard.
All: Please...

This was first done on All Saints'Day as a class meditation, but it has since been used as a follow up to lessons on various themes to do with living as God wants us to.

EVERY DAY IS GOD'S DAY

This was an end of the summer term celebration, involving 120 children aged 5-9. There were eleven classes of children meeting weekly and each class had, the week previous to the celebration, made part of a 6ft by 6ft picture of sky, mountains, hills and fields, a house, animals, birds, sea fish, seaside, and people. Each class also produced a prayer about their bit of the picture. There was close co-operation among the catechists so that everything was in proportion, more or less, and the co-ordinator gave detailed instructions about size. The youngest children coped with the sky, a huge sun and a cotton wool cloud. The six-year-olds did the sea with blue tissue and sellophane waves and lots of fish and so on, with the nines responsible for people and animals.

The catechists had prepared a balloon for each child, and written in permanent felt pen, 'Every day is God's day'. We found it best to blow the balloon half-way up, hold it, write on it and let it down again. Writing on them when they were not inflated resulted in very pale lettering when the balloons were blown up.

Hymn: 'Morning has broken...' (Celebration Hymnal No. 196)

Introduction: During the year, we've done a lot together, we've worked, prayed and celebrated and now before we break up we've all come together to think about the holidays that we're just beginning.
We often think about God being with us at home, in church and at Saturday school and this morning we're going to think about him being with us wherever we go. No matter where we go on holiday, God is there with us.

Everyone made a bit of a picture last week and today we're going to put all the bits together and make one huge holiday picture. Before the five-year-olds put their sky up, we'll sing.

Hymn: 'All creation bless the Lord...' Verse 1 only. (Celebration Hymnal No.3)

The sky was put up with a thinking prayer about the sun.
The mountains and hills were fixed immediately against the sky.

Prayer: We thank you God for the sun that warms us and makes everything grow. We thank you for the mountains and hills we can climb and run down.

Hymn: 'Winds and breezes bless the Lord... (Verse 2)

Flowers and grass and fields went up next. A house was put in position.

Prayer: We thank you for the flowers which make our world full of colour, and which we can pick to make our homes look attractive.

Hymn: 'Night and daytime bless the Lord...'

Sand, pebbles, beach toys and sandcastles went up with this prayer:

Prayer: We praise you, God, for sand, soft and yellow.

The sea and fish were put next to the sand and squared the picture off.

Prayer: We praise you, God, and thank you for all the different kinds of fish you put into the sea; all the plain ones and all those which are beautiful with colours.

Hymn: 'Springs and rivers bless the Lord...'

Big trees with leaves made by the class and small trees by individuals were added.

Prayer: We praise you, God, for trees that give us shade. We praise you for fruit trees and for trees that are useful for furniture.

Birds, aeroplanes and a helicopter decorated the sky.

Prayer: We thank you, God, for the birds which fly in the sky and rest on the trees. We also thank you for helping men to create planes and helicopters which carry people round the world.

Hymn: 'Let God's people bless the Lord...'

People were dotted about the picture, animals completed it.

Prayer: We thank you, Lord, for all the people you
made and for all the animals. We thank you
especially for the people we know and the animals we have at home.

Give the children a quick guided tour through
the picture they have made, commenting briefly
on the different aspects and allowing short
spaces for prayer.

Hymn: (to the tune of 'Sing Hosanna'.)
You're with us in our hearts while we're playing.
You're with us in our hearts always.
You're with us in our hearts while we're playing.
While we're playing on our holidays.
Sing hosanna...

You're with us in our hearts when we travel.
You're with us in our hearts always.
You're with us in our hearts when we travel.
When we travel on our holidays.
Sing hosanna....

Every day of our lives you are with us.
Every day of our lives you're here.
Every day of our lives you are with us.
You'll be with us on our holidays.
Sing hosanna...

It is often useful to have a quiet reading on the
theme of the celebration. The psalms offer
plenty of scope. We used Psalm 138, adapted
from 'Praise' with some verses (marked with
asterisks) composed for the occasion. Two nine-
year-olds alternated reading the verses.

Psalm: You know me, Lord, so very well,
you know when I get up.
You know when I go back to sleep,

you know each thing I do.

You know what I am going to say
before I even speak!
You are always close to me.
You're wonderful, O Lord.

*During these holidays
let me stay close to you.
Wherever I go, you'll be there.
May I not forget you.

So if I climbed the highest hill,
you would be there with me.
And if I swam beneath the waves,
you'd still be there with me.

*If I see animals in the woods,
or cattle on the hillsides,
let me remember they belong to you, Lord.
For you made them.

*If I see birds up in the trees,
let me remember you know each one,
just as you know me.

*Whenever I see a living thing
out in the fields,
let me think of you.
You made them and will never
forget any of them.
And you do not forget anyone.

*During the holidays
let me stay close to you.
Wherever I go, you'll be there.
May I not forget you.

Final Hymn: The children chose one of the hymns to
sing.

Each child was given a balloon with its special message and a holiday prayer to say alone or with the family as a reminder of God's love for him/her.

Holiday Prayer:
　　　　During these holidays
　　　　let us stay close to you, Lord.
　　　　Wherever we go, you'll be there.
　　　　May we not forget you.

　　　　Every day, school days and holidays,
　　　　weekdays and Sundays,
　　　　every day is a present to us from God.
　　　　Every day is God's day
　　　　given to us to use.

CHAPTER 6

Celebrating the Liturgy of the Word

We have found that a Liturgy of the Word monthly, a special family Mass in church monthly and two ordinary Masses make a useful pattern so that the children don't lose touch with the normal way of worshipping with their parents and the other adults.

The Directory on Children's Masses encourages us to have separate Liturgies of the Word for children as one way of leading them into deeper involvement in the Eucharist. It is possible to have a separate Liturgy of the Word on Sundays, when children of school age (it should not be a crèche for under-fives) have an adapted liturgy and join the congregation at the Offertory.

This needs a bit of organisation, e.g. someone reliable to come and tell the catechists or parents when the adults are beginning the Creed, so that the children's liturgy can be smoothly rounded off and the children are not rushed into church.

Sometimes the children begin in church and have a procession to the room where they will pray, with the Bible or Missal carried solemnly. But we found that it gave a longer time for the Liturgy of the Word if the children went straight into the hall and we began our liturgy at the same time as the adults began theirs.

It is good to have a visual focus when the children come in: a table on which are a Bible and candles, or an empty table waiting for these to be carried there in procession; a board with the key theme of the Mass written up, e.g. 'Father, forgive them,' or, 'The Lord is near.' Sometimes a picture of flowers or something made by one of the classes would be good. Above all there should be a feeling that the room is expectant, waiting for something important to occur. If there are no chairs, then perhaps blankets or rugs might be available.

The structure should be such that it is recognisably the same as the adults' liturgy. The reading, whenever possible, should be that of the day, simplified if necessary; with two readings, especially if the link is clear.

Each child should have a stencilled sheet with the hymns and prayers on it and sometimes a visual and/or a quiz; suggestions for a table decoration, e.g. a crown for the feast of Christ the King to be used at home. This is an attempt to communicate with the rest of the family and to carry the liturgy back to their homes. It does not need to be elaborate, but it should not become too much of a routine.

THE PATTERN

Opening Hymn: if possible on the theme of the liturgy.

Penance Rite: This is often worked out by one class of children beforehand and sometimes comes after the Reading(s).

Procession: with Bible and candles to a table covered with a white cloth. Often some children process while others say a prayer.

Reading(s): We almost always stick to the ones of the Sunday, using Alan Dale's simplification if necessary.

Homily: Comment by a child or children. This would

need some guidance/support from the teacher/ catechist. Visuals are often used.

Creed: The Creed is sometimes said. Occasionally a home-made Creed is used, based on the Mass theme. It is possible to make up a Creed with a class of children during a lesson which can then be used for such liturgies.

Bidding Prayers: These are usually spontaneous from the children and introduced by the catechist.

Final Hymn.

'STAY WITH ME
THAT I MAY HELP YOU GROW'

The focal point of this liturgy was a big picture of a tree. One group had drawn and cut out people that they had stuck round the tree after the Gospel reading.

The catechist explained that the people were attracted to the tree by its beauty and shade, and talked about it growing from a tiny seed.

Hymn: All things bright and beautiful,
all creatures great and small,
all things wise and wonderful,
the Lord God made them all.

Each little flower that opens,
each little bird that sings,
he made their glowing colours,
he made their tiny wings.

Chorus: All things bright ...

The purple-headed mountain,
the river running by,
the sunset and the morning,
that brightens up the sky.

Chorus: All things bright ...

(Celebration Hymnal No.13)

Bible procession: Some children, carrying the Bible and
candles, process to a table covered with a white
cloth while everyone else prays aloud.
Catechist: Let us pray:
All: Lord God, we have come together to praise and
thank you.
We have come together to listen to your Word.
Help us, your people, as we get ready to listen
to you.
You speak in the words of your Son, who is the
Word of God. Amen.

Reading: from the Book of Ezechiel 17:22-24

Reading: from St Mark's Gospel 4:26-34

Penitential Rite: Lord have mercy. Christ have mercy.
Lord have mercy.

Homily: Thinking about the tree growing from a tiny

seed and how people were attracted to the tree
by its beauty and shade.

Hymn: Even though my time has not yet come,
I shall tell you where this wine came from.
I'm the holy vine that gave you this wine
only as a sign of love.

So if you decide to come to me,
I will make you branches of this tree,
so that you will be always close to me.
Then we all will be one vine.

Without me you really can't be good,
You don't even do the things you should.
For when branches die and their leaves turn dry,
they can't ever give us fruit.

God our Father will then cut away
all the branches that cannot display
any useful fruit or a hopeful shoot
coming from the root below.

So join hands with me and don't let go.
Stay with me that I may help you grow
in my love and grace. Then, in every place,
men will see my face in yours.
        (From Advent to Easter)

Bidding Prayers: Think about yourself growing in
Christ's love, growing so much in love that
people want to be your friend; come to you for
help. Write your name on the tree. Think of the
things you like to be - things like: brave, sharing, forgiving, friendly, generous, kind, cheer-
ful - things which make us more like Jesus.
Write these on the branches and pray that you
will be so like Jesus that people will want to be
your friend.

FEAST OF CHRIST THE KING

Hymn: Christ be beside me,
Christ be before me,
Christ be behind me,
King of my heart.
Christ be within me,
Christ be below me,
Christ be above me,
never to part.

Christ at my right hand,
Christ at my left hand,
Christ all around me,
shield in the strife.
Christ in my sleeping,
Christ in my sitting,
Christ in my rising,
light of my life.

Christ be in all hearts,
thinking about me,
Christ be in all tongues
telling of me.
Christ be the vision
in eyes that see me,
in ears that hear me,

Christ ever be.

(Celebration Hymnal No.41)

Penitential Rite:

Catechist: Let us think about what we have done wrong
on purpose.

All:　Lord have mercy. Christ have mercy.
Lord have mercy.

Bible Procession:

Catechist: Let us pray:

All:　Lord God, we have come together to praise
and thank you.
We have come together to listen to your word.
Help us, your people, as we get ready to listen
to you.
You speak in the words of your Son, who is the
Word of God. Amen.

Reading: Daniel 7:

Introduction: This reading is part of a sort of dream
that Daniel had about the Son of Man coming to
be King of the World. 'Son of Man' was one of
the names given to the one who was to be sent
by God to show the world how much God loves
us. We call the Son of Man, Jesus Christ, our
Lord.
Daniel writes:
When I was lying on my bed at night,
I had a strange dream or vision;
this is what I saw:
The Son of Man,
brought by the clouds of heaven,
came to the Everlasting God
and was presented to him.

The Son of Man was crowned king,
with all the glory and honour of a great king,

he was in charge of the whole world
and his power would last for ever.
His kingdom will always be here
and will never be destroyed.

Reading: from St John's Gospel 18:28-31 (From 'New
World' by Alan Dale)

Introduction: This reading is from St John's Gospel
and describes how, after Jesus' arrest, he is
taken before Pilate who has the power to set
him free or to have him killed. Pilate speaks
to Jesus: (This is read as a dialogue between
Jesus and Pilate.)

Pilate: 'So you're the Jewish King, are you?'

Jesus: 'Are those your own words? Or are you just
repeating what other people have told you?'

Pilate: 'Do I look like a Jew! You've been brought
here by your own leaders. What have you been
up to?'

Jesus: 'I'm no nationalist. My men would have been
out on the streets fighting, if I were—they
wouldn't have let me be arrested so easily. My
"kingdom" has nothing to do with that sort of
thing.'

Pilate: 'So you are a "king" then.'

Jesus: 'The word is yours. I was born to defend the
truth. Anybody who cares for the truth knows
what I am talking about.'

Hymn: (To the tune of 'Give me Joy in my Heart...')
Christ the King is our Lord, keep us serving,
Christ the King, is our Lord we know,
Christ the King is our Lord keep us serving,
Keep us serving 'till the end of day.
Chorus: Sing hosanna! Sing hosanna!
Sing hosanna to the King of Kings!

Sing hosanna! Sing hosanna! Sing
hosanna to the King!

Christ is King of our hearts, keep us loving,
Christ is King of our hearts, we know.
Christ is King of our hearts, keep us loving,
Keep us loving 'till the end of day.
Chorus: Sing hosanna! ....

Christ is King of the world, keep us praising,
Christ is King of the world, we know.
Christ is King of the world, keep us praising,
Keep us praising 'till the end of day.
Chorus: Sing hosanna! ....

(Celebration Hymnal No. 84)

Creed:

Bidding Prayers:

Hymn:

At the bottom of the stencilled sheet, which each
child was given at the beginning of the liturgy, a big
outline of a crown was drawn. Before joining the adults
at Mass the catechist said to the children:
You may like to colour the crown shape and stick coloured foil on to make jewels. (This could be done there
and then, time permitting, or at home.)
If you cut the crown out and join the ends you can stand
it on a table at a family meal today. Put your candle,
which you will be given on your way out, in the crown to
remind you that today is the feast of Christ the King.
Perhaps you can say or sing one of the hymns on your
sheet of paper as a beginning to that meal.

'I NEVER STOP LOVING YOU'

Liturgy of the Word based on the Gospel Story of the Prodigal Son.

Hymn:

Penance Rite: Worked out by one of the classes beforehand.

> For the times we have been unkind, Lord, have mercy.
> For the times we have been selfish, Lord, have mercy.

> For the times we have not thought about our parents, Lord, have mercy.

Procession:

Reading: Luke 15:11-32

Homily: Each of five groups contributed something visual. Group one, brought two halves of a circle with the words, 'Forgiving is coming together.' Group two, drew hands clasped in friendship. Group three, split the word FOR GIVING and spoke about forgiving meaning that we are 'for giving' to others; they spoke of our love and friendship as being something to share. Group four, drew 'smiley' faces and told the whole group that forgiving makes us happy.
Group five, had a picture of people which they had cut up and then pieced together again. This was to illustrate that when we hurt people, we are separate; but when we forgive we come together.

> Afterwards the visuals were put up and explained by the classes and we sang a hymn about making peace.

Hymn: 'Making Peace'.
        This was taken from Christiane Brusselmans'
        record, 'We Celebrate the Eucharist'.

BECOMING MORE LIKE JESUS

Liturgy of the Word based on John 15:9-11.

Hymn:

Procession: Some of the children, carrying a Bible and
        candles, processed to a table covered with a
        white cloth. The others said the following
        prayer:
        Lord God, we have come together to praise and
        thank you.
        We have come together to listen to your Word.
        Help us, your people, as we get ready to listen
        to you. You speak the words of your Son, who
        is the Word of God.   Amen.

Reading: John 15:9-11

Homily: Each child was given a piece of paper. On one
        side was written, 'Alleluia! Love one another
        as I have loved you,' and on the other, 'God,
        our Father, please help ... to be more like
        Jesus, your Son.' Each child wrote her/his
        name in the space after 'please help...' and the
        papers were collected, shuffled and given out,
        so that each one had the name of someone to
        pray for. If there was time each child said her/
        his own name out loud so that the person who
        had her/his name on their bit of paper could be
        sure to remember what she/he looked like. If

time was short they simply took the paper home as a reminder to pray for others and for that named person in particular.

Hymn:

TELL THE GOOD NEWS TO THE WHOLE WORLD

Liturgy of the Word based on the choosing of the twelve apostles.

Introduction: The focal point was twelve unlit, different looking candles which could be seen by all the children. Hanging on the wall, clearly written were the names of the twelve apostles. The liturgy began with a brief explanation that the candles represented the apostles and that, after the Gospel reading, as each candle was lit, the children would call out the name of the apostle i.e. candle one, first apostle etc.

Hymn: 'God's Spirit is in my heart,...' Celebration Hymnal No. 99.

Penance Rite:

Procession:

Reading: Matthew 9:36-10:8

Homily: After the Gospel, the children all read aloud together the apostles' names slowly and a candle was lit as each name was called. When these were all alight, the catechist asked why each candle was different and this led to talking about how people do things differently, by word, by work, by helping. A discussion started about

71

how everybody passes on God's love in their own special way and how God needs us all if his love is to be passed on to the whole world. Jesus chose some apostles who were clever, others who were not clever, some who were rich, others poorer; each one was needed to do his part in changing the world into the kingdom of God.

Kiss of Peace: This was given to show that everyone wants to be like the apostles in extending Christ's kingdom of love and peace.

Hymn: 'Let's make peace...' Folk Hymnal Vol.1 No.2)

On the stencilled sheet which each child had been given, were the names of the twelve apostles written round the edge.

Toward the bottom of the page was a heading: 'They were sent by Jesus to tell everyone the Good News.'

Under this heading was written: 'We tell the Good News, not in words but in the way we live.'

A space was left so that the children could fill in ways in which they might bring the Good News into the world and draw themselves as apostles of today.

PEACE BE WITH YOU

Liturgy of the Word based on John 20:19-22 and Acts 2

Introduction: Jesus says, 'Peace be with you' to the apostles and the apostles, in Acts, tell the world that the Spirit of Jesus is with them.

Hymn: 'Pass it on...' (Celebration Hymnal No.210) or 'Shalom...' (Celebration Hymnal No. 276)

Reading: St John 20:19-22
Catechist: Jesus says 'Peace be with you'.

Reading: Acts 2
Catechist: The apostles tell everyone that the Spirit
is with them.

Homily: Thinking silently about the readings.

Creed: (Home-made Creed, based on the Liturgy of
the Word.)
We believe in God, the Father, creator of heav-
en and earth, who loves us and sends us the
Spirit of Love.
We believe in Jesus Christ, his only Son, our
Lord, who gives us peace and love.
We believe in the Holy Spirit, the giver of life,
who is with us always to help us to love like
Jesus.
We believe in the Catholic Church,
a sign in the world of peace and love.   Amen.

Penance Rite: This could follow the creed, using the
phrases that occur in it:
Lord, you love us and send us the Spirit of Love,
Lord, have mercy.
Lord, you came to bring us peace and love,
Christ, have mercy.
Lord, you ask us to be a sign of love and peace
in our world.
Lord, have mercy.

Bidding Prayers: Before the Bidding Prayers, the catechist talks about the Spirit of Jesus being within
us always, helping us to be what God has made
us to be: sharing, forgiving, helpful, thoughtful,
peace-making.
The older children listed these qualities while
the younger ones, and those who wanted, drew
themselves smiling as a sign that they were
ready to share the joy of the Spirit with those

they met.

If there has been an opportunity during the lesson in which the Liturgy was prepared, the older children could have made large decorative posters with a quality of the Spirit on each. While the catechist explains how the Spirit helps us to be forgiving etc. each child helps to hang his/her poster up at the appropriate time. The younger children could have drawn themselves smiling and their drawings could be stuck on a big piece of paper on the wall.

Hymn:

CHAPTER 7

Basic Preparation for Children's Liturgies

INFORMING THE PARISH

It is obviously important for the adults in a parish, particularly those without young children, to understand when there is a separate Liturgy of the Word for children. Sometimes a note can be put into the parish newsletter the previous Sunday to reinforce the publicity which the priest will give from the pulpit.

Below is the text of a note given out at regular intervals in our own and other parishes:

'On the third Sunday of each month there is a Liturgy of the Word in the church hall for any children who wish to participate. Some of the catechists plan and lead the celebration which takes place at the same time as the Liturgy of the Word for adults in church. The pattern of the children's celebration is usually as follows: An opening hymn; a suitable examination of conscience and Penance Rite, which is often worked out in class with the children beforehand; a procession with the Bible and candles; the Sunday readings, simplified if need be; a brief homily; sometimes the Creed; Bidding Prayers from the children and a final hymn.

'The pattern may vary but the intention is to make the Word of God more relevant to children and to give them the opportunity to be more deeply involved, through specially chosen hymns, through the Bidding Prayers etc. By these means the catechists believe they are helping the children to enter more deeply into the mystery of the Mass.

'The children who wish to take part should go straight to the hall at .... time and will rejoin their families later, at the Offertory.'

Sometimes we amplify the explanation given above from 'The Usual Pattern of Children's Liturgies' (See pp 61-62)

INVOLVING THE CHILDREN

To involve children in preparing liturgies, the catechist needs to be there to guide and advise and comment on what they are doing, otherwise the liturgy can become disjointed. It is useful to talk around the idea before suggesting that the children get down to preparing it, so that they deepen their understanding of what they are doing. It is to be 'their' liturgy and 'their' work; the catechist is there in an enabling capacity, and it is certainly needed. It is important to give the children time to work on the given theme. If it is during Saturday classes they may need two lesson times to produce what they feel is useful. This is not wasted time, but time of praying and thinking about the Word of God.

If a child is going to produce a homily or comment on the readings, make sure that he/she has prepared it well. Talk to him well beforehand about the readings and listen to his ideas. Jot down for him what seem to be the points he wants to get over. Guide him when he seems to be picking up the Scripture incorrectly. Above all, make sure that before he actually does the 'homily' in front of the children, he is happy about it. Listen to him yourself, first, and encourage him.

It is quite possible and often much more effective in R.E. teaching and experience to let the children compose a creed of their own - i.e. one class working on the reading and drawing out from it what beliefs it portrays or evokes in them. As thoughts come to their minds they can be written up on the board and rephrased if necessary, by the teacher/catechist so that the creed reads easily and meaningfully. It can then be stencilled for use at the children's liturgy.

IN A SCHOOL SITUATION

With all these liturgies of the Word, it is perfectly possible, in a school situation, to adapt them easily to a lesson time. They are all learning experiences and a deepening of the children's relationship with Jesus. They do not have to precede a Eucharistic celebration, but can stand on their own.

Also in a school situation several lessons can go into preparation for the liturgy. The older the children, the more understanding can go into this. There is too, more opportunity for the children to compose their own prayers and psalms. These could be stencilled in time for the celebration, so that they can all share fully in it.

PREPARING READERS

When a child is asked to read in front of any group of people, but particularly in a church, he/she must feel completely confident, sure of himself and familiar with what he has to read. This does not mean over-rehearsing as this can cause an uninteresting and boring reading. It is a case of the teacher/catechist being able to pinpoint the moment when a particular child is sufficiently confident.

An important fact to keep in mind when preparing readers, is that, generally speaking, a nervous child will read more quickly than usual. To read in church or hall, a slower speed is needed, so that the sound reaches all parts without a time lag, which causes an echo. The more confident the child, the more able he will be to control the speed at which he reads. It is also true to say, that a nervous child will read in a soft and inaudible voice, therefore practice is important, both informally and formally where the reading will actually take place.

When preparing a reading, it is helpful to write it out clearly (typed if possible) in sense lines which almost invariably produce natural pauses. (See example on p.80) Try not to cover the page with directions or underlinings as these are unnecessary once the child is familiar with the reading, and they can also cause a lot of distraction. Whoever is responsible for practising the reader should also have a copy so that they can work together, noticing the difficult words and generally becoming familiar with the text.

In the beginning practise the reading in the child's home or in the classroom rather than in the church or hall. The child will be less nervous and feel more at ease. Encourage him/her to hold his/her head up so that you can see his face and lips. After two or three practices in this situation, move to the church or hall and do exactly the same routine, but tell the child that you will stand in different places to make sure that you can hear him/her. Praise the reader freely, particularly as his/her voice becomes clearer and more relaxed. Talk to him about the text and how he feels about reading it in church now he has tried it. Once you are sure he is happy, then go ahead, but don't pressurise a child into reading because he has a good voice or because you like the way he reads. He must feel at ease also. It is perhaps useful to mention here that, from experience, I have found that it is not always only the children who have clear, loud voices who can read well in church. Sometimes an apparently shy or retiring child, with enough encouragement, can read simply beautifully and enjoy it. These children often get overlooked but enjoy the challenge and get a tremendous thrill from sharing what the others are doing.

When practising in the church, make sure that the reader feels completely at home with the lectern (if it is used) and the microphone. Explain that everyone needs to hear what he is reading, even the mother with the baby on the back row. This will encourage voice projection and help him to remember to speak clearly. To be as relaxed as possible, let the reader practice walking to and from the lectern, putting down the paper quietly, pausing to wait for the church to settle down, and assuring him that you will give him the signal to start. Let him feel that you will be hear him in case of any emergency, such as sudden panic, but by no means whisper directions whilst he is reading as it is likely to throw any reader, however confident. If the parents are co-operative, let the child take home the text to practise, but once again, do not let the child become bored with it.

On the actual day, make sure that the child contacts you before the Liturgy to check that he has the reading with him. If not, give him yours, and be sure you have an extra copy. Reassure him that before he actually starts to read, you will see that the microphone is at the right height. This is very important if the priest has already used it, as the chances are, he will have it higher than the child needs it.

When it comes to Bidding Prayers, the same procedure can be used, but although they may only be short prayers, never ask a child to read 'off the cuff' however

confident you may think they are. Their reaction would
be the same as yours or mine, and the chances are
they would not be heard. If a child does not turn up for
whatever reason, read the prayer yourself, or alterna-
tively, provide each child with two prayers - their own
and the one that follows - so that should someone be
absent, you are covered. By making sure you see the
readers before Mass, you can sort out which prayer or
prayers they are to read. Encourage them to leave a
reasonable pause between the end of the prayer and
'Lord hear us', to give people the chance to actually
pray, as so often there is no time given.

If these guidelines are followed, there should not be
too many problems. It is obvious that each parish
teacher and catechist will have their own ideas and
each parish will differ as to the problems caused by
amplification systems etc., but generally speaking, the
ideas mentioned above have proved successful.

EXAMPLE OF SENSE LINES

Mark 4:26-34 written out for readers in
sense and pause lines:

Jesus went on to say
'The kingdom of God is like this.
A man scatters seed in his field.
He sleeps at night,
is up and about during the day,
and all the while
the seeds are sprouting and growing.
Yet he does not know how it happens.
The soil itself makes the plants grow and bear fruit;
first the tender stalk appears
then the ear,
and finally the ear full of corn.
When the corn is ripe,
the man starts cutting it with his sickle,

because the harvest time has come.

'What shall we say the Kingdom of God is like?'asked
Jesus.
What parable shall we use to explain it?
It is like this.
A man takes a mustard seed,
the smallest seed in the world,
and plants it in the ground.
After a while it grows up
and becomes the biggest of all plants.
It puts out such large branches
that the birds come
and make their nests in its shade.'

USEFUL BOOKS

Praise   Songs and poems from the Bible retold for
children
by A J McCallen
Collins Liturgical Publications
ISBN 0 00 599621 10

Listen   by A J McCallen
Collins Liturgical Publications
ISBN 0 00 599528 X

Winding Quest
by Alan T Dale
Oxford University Press
ISBN 0 19 833828 7

New World
by Alan T Dale
Oxford University Press
ISBN 0 19 833834 1

Tools for Meditation
by J de Rooy SJ
The Grail
ISBN 0 901829 29 3

Directory on Children's Masses
The Incorporated Catholic Truth Society, London

Advent to Easter Short musical plays for children
by Denis O'Gorman
The Grail
ISBN 0 901829 25 0

We Celebrate the Eucharist
Coordinated Components: Pupil's Book. Guidelines for
Parents and Catechists. Program Director's Manual.

Celebrations. Record
        by Christiane Brusselmans & Brian A Haggerty
        Silver Burdett Co.
        ISBN 0 382 00015 3 Guidelines
        ISBN 0 382 00018 8 Record

Your Word is Near
        by Huub Oosterhuis
        Paulist Press - obtainable in UK from Fowler
        Wright Books Ltd, Leominster Hereford
        ISBN 0 8091 1775 4

20th Century Folk Hymnal vols 1 and 2
People's copy
        Compiled by Kevin Mayhew
        Palm Tree Press, Leigh on Sea Essex
        ISBN 0 905725 27 1 (vol 1) 0 905725 22 0 (vol 2)

Celebration Hymnal
        Mayhew McCrimmon Ltd
        ISBN 0 85597 094 4

Twenty-Four Psalms & a Canticle
        The Grail

Thirty Psalms & Two Canticles
        The Grail